RESS, July 4, 1776.

of the thirteen united States of America,

When in the Course of human events, it becomes necessary for one people to dissolve the political bands which have connected them with another, and to assume among the powers of the earth, the separate and equal station to which the Laws of Nature and of Nature's God entitle them, a decent respect to the opinions of mankind requires that they should declare the causes which impel them to the separation.

We hold these truths to be self-evident, that all men are created equal, that they are endowed by their Creator with certain unalienable Rights, that among these are Life, Liberty and the pursuit of Happiness.—That to secure these rights, Governments are instituted among Men, deriving their just powers from the consent of the governed,—That whenever any Form of Government becomes destructive of these ends, it is the Right of the People to alter or to abolish it, and to institute new Government, laying its foundation on such principles and organizing its powers in such form, as to them shall seem most likely to effect their Safety and Happiness. Prudence, indeed, will dictate that Governments long established should not be changed for light and transient causes; and accordingly all experience hath shewn, that mankind are more disposed to suffer, while evils are sufferable, than to right themselves by abolishing the forms to which they are accustomed. But when a long train of abuses and usurpations, pursuing invariably the same Object evinces a design to reduce them under absolute Despotism, it is their right, it is their duty, to throw off such Government, and to provide new Guards for their future security.—Such has been the patient sufferance of these Colonies; and such is now the necessity which constrains them to alter their former Systems of Government. The history of the present King of Great Britain is a history of repeated injuries and usurpations, all having in direct object the establishment of an absolute Tyranny over these States. To prove this, let Facts be submitted to a candid world.

He has refused his Assent to Laws, the most wholesome and necessary for the public good.

He has forbidden his Governors to pass Laws of immediate and pressing importance, unless suspended in their operation till his Assent should be obtained; and when so suspended, he has utterly neglected to attend to them.

He has refused to pass other Laws for the accommodation of large districts of people, unless those people would relinquish the right of Representation in the Legislature, a right inestimable to them and formidable to tyrants only.

He has called together legislative bodies at places unusual, uncomfortable, and distant from the depository of their public Records, for the sole purpose of fatiguing them into compliance with his measures.

He has dissolved Representative Houses repeatedly, for opposing with manly firmness his invasions on the rights of the people.

He has refused for a long time, after such dissolutions, to cause others to be elected; whereby the Legislative powers, incapable of Annihilation, have returned to the People at large for their exercise; the State remaining in the mean time exposed to all the dangers of invasion from without, and convulsions within.

He has endeavoured to prevent the population of these States; for that purpose obstructing the Laws for Naturalization of Foreigners; refusing to pass others to encourage their migrations hither, and raising the conditions of new Appropriations of Lands.

He has obstructed the Administration of Justice, by refusing his Assent to Laws for establishing Judiciary powers.

He has made Judges dependent on his Will alone, for the tenure of their offices,

The Declaration of Independence
from A to Z

By Catherine L. Osornio
Paintings by Layne Johnson

PELICAN PUBLISHING COMPANY
GRETNA 2010

To my family and friends for all their support, patience, and prayers; and to all who appreciate what it means to be free. —C. O.

Thanks to all the Colonial artists who have come before us. Without the likes of Charles Willson Peale, John Singleton Copley, John Trumbull, and Gilbert Stuart, we would not have the visual references of the Founding Fathers that we have today. I tip my tricorn to them! —L. J.

Copyright © 2010
By Catherine L. Osornio

Paintings copyright © 2010
By Layne Johnson
All rights reserved

The word "Pelican" and the depiction of a pelican are trademarks of Pelican Publishing Company, Inc., and are registered in the U.S. Patent and Trademark Office.

Library of Congress Cataloging-in-Publication Data

Osornio, Catherine L.
  The Declaration of Independence from A to Z / by Catherine L. Osornio ; illustrated by Layne Johnson.
       p. cm.
  ISBN 978-1-58980-676-4 (hardcover : alk. paper) 1. United States. Declaration of Independence—Juvenile literature. 2. United States—Politics and government—1775-1783—Juvenile literature. 3. Alphabet books—Juvenile literature. I. Johnson, Layne, ill. II. Title.
  E221.O86 2010
  973.3'13—dc22
                                  2009030282

Printed in Malaysia
Published by Pelican Publishing Company, Inc.
1000 Burmaster Street, Gretna, Louisiana 70053

A is for America.

America was originally a group of thirteen colonies along eastern North America. The Colonies were ruled by King George III of England who lived far across the sea.

B is for Boston Tea Party.

King George made the Colonists pay extra taxes for goods and services. He believed he could tax them on anything, including their tea. The Colonists had no one in the British government to represent them.

One December night in 1773, a group of men and boys met at Boston Harbor. They were dressed like Mohawk Indians. Their mission was to destroy all the tea aboard three British ships. Careful not to cause any other damage, the group dumped the tea into the harbor. The event was called the Boston Tea Party.

C is for Continental Congress.

King George was angry, especially with the people of Boston. He made some new rules. There would be no more town meetings, and Boston Harbor would be closed until the tea was paid for. Soldiers were sent from Britain to America and were housed in people's homes without permission.

The Continental Congress was formed in September of 1774 at Carpenters' Hall in Philadelphia to defend the rights of the Colonists.

D is for Delegates.

Fifty-five representatives, or delegates, from the Colonies met for seven weeks. Most delegates wanted peace. Some wanted war to protect their liberties. Congress sent a letter to King George asking that Americans be given the same rights as those in England.

E is for Enemy.

King George did not accept Congress's letter. He declared Massachusetts to be in rebellion and wanted Samuel Adams and John Hancock of Boston arrested. The king called these men enemies of England, because he felt they would hurt his country.

F is for Fight.

The British Redcoats marched to Lexington looking for the rebel leaders. They met American soldiers called Minutemen. A fight started. Eight Americans died.

The Redcoats marched to Concord looking for hidden gunpowder. Minutemen came from other towns and villages. Paul Revere and William Dawes had warned them that the British were coming. Another fight broke out. This time the British ran back to Boston in fear.

G is for Grievances.

The grievances, or complaints, against the king grew. He cut off American trade with other countries. He took away a person's right to a trial by jury and the charters the Colonists used to govern themselves. These actions made the people angrier.

H is for John Hancock.

John Hancock joined the other delegates in Philadelphia in May of 1775 to start up the Second Continental Congress. He served as president. Congress again tried to make peace with England but with no success.

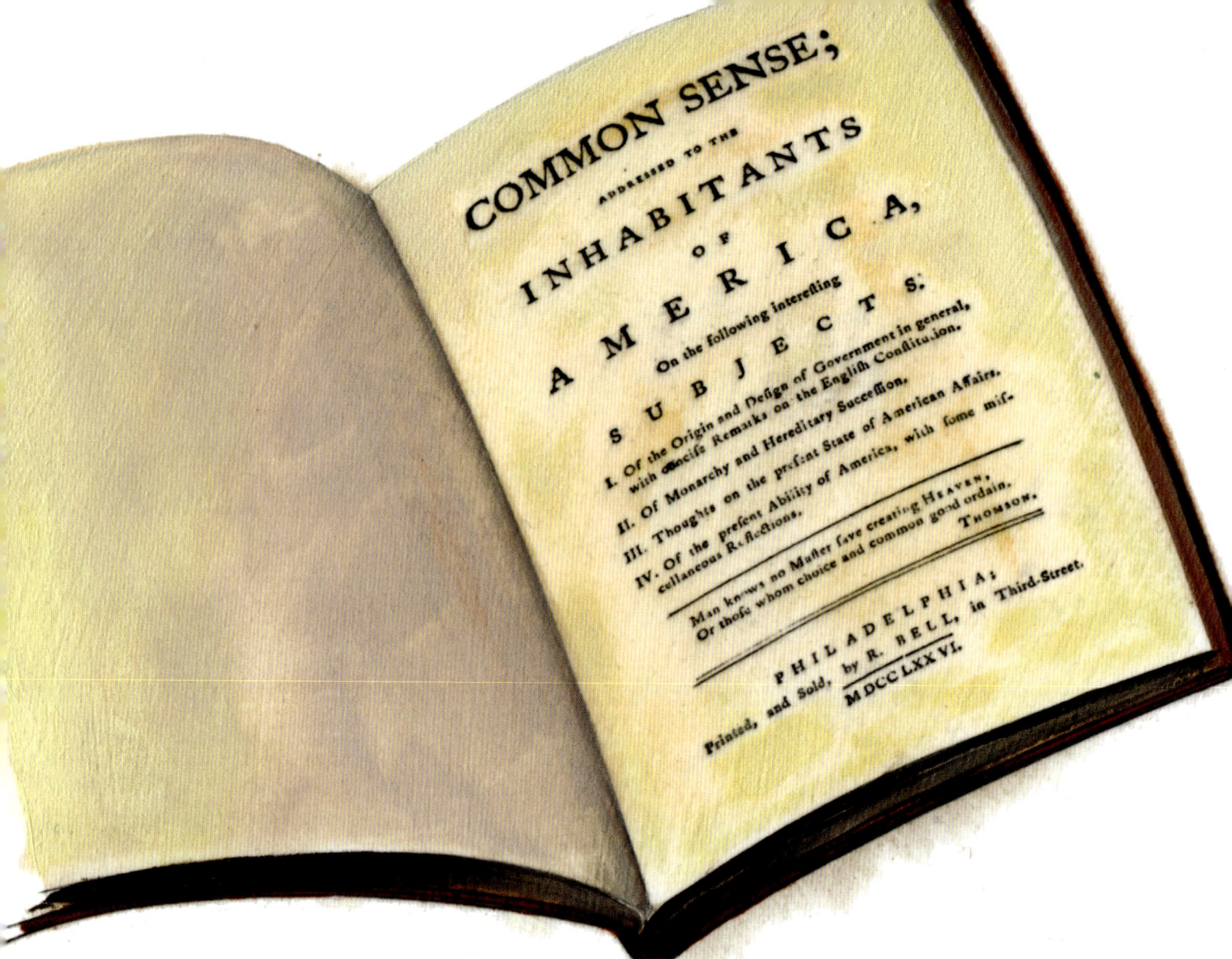

I is for Independence.

A pamphlet came out in January of 1776 called "Common Sense." It was written by Thomas Paine and showed the Colonists how it was *common sense* to seek independence from England. Within the first three months, one copy was sold for about every sixteen people in the Colonies.

Richard Henry Lee of Virginia proposed that Congress take a vote for independence. Since many delegates needed to speak with the citizens back home, they agreed to meet in early July of 1776 to vote.

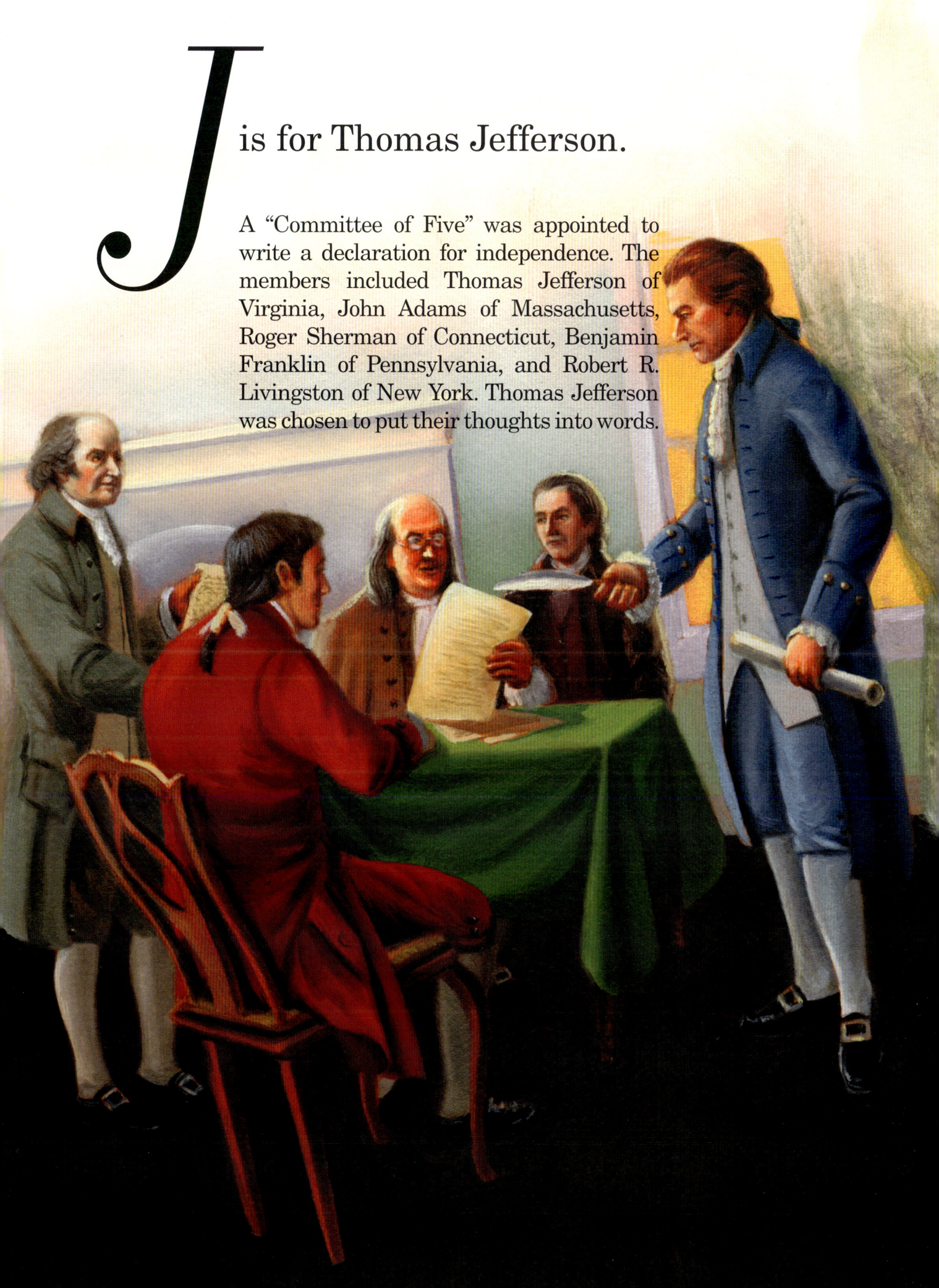

J is for Thomas Jefferson.

A "Committee of Five" was appointed to write a declaration for independence. The members included Thomas Jefferson of Virginia, John Adams of Massachusetts, Roger Sherman of Connecticut, Benjamin Franklin of Pennsylvania, and Robert R. Livingston of New York. Thomas Jefferson was chosen to put their thoughts into words.

K is for Keynote.

The keynote, or main message, of the Declaration was to tell the world why America should separate from England and create its own government. Twenty-seven grievances were written against the king.

L is for Life, Liberty, and the Pursuit of Happiness.

The Declaration stated that people were "endowed by their Creator with certain unalienable Rights, that among these are Life, Liberty and the pursuit of Happiness." If a government acted in a way to destroy these rights, then it was the right of the people to change that government.

M is for Majority.

Congress was shown the document on July 2. After making changes, the delegates voted. The majority, or largest number of delegates, accepted the rewritten Declaration of Independence on July 4, 1776.

N is for Nation.

John Hancock, the president of Congress, and Charles Thomson, the secretary of Congress, were the only ones to sign the document that day. With their signatures, they declared that a new nation was born.

O is for Oath.

The last line of the Declaration was an oath, or promise:

"And for the support of this Declaration, with a firm reliance on the protection of Divine Providence, we mutually pledge to each other our Lives, our Fortunes and our Sacred Honor."

P is for Proclaim.

On July 8, the Declaration was read to large crowds in Philadelphia. The old state house bell, later named the Liberty Bell, was rung. On it were words from the Bible, "PROCLAIM Liberty throughout all the land unto all inhabitants thereof" (Leviticus 25:10).

Q is for Quill.

A large bird feather is called a quill. These feathers made excellent pens when the ends were sharpened and the points dipped into ink. A quill pen was used to write and sign the Declaration.

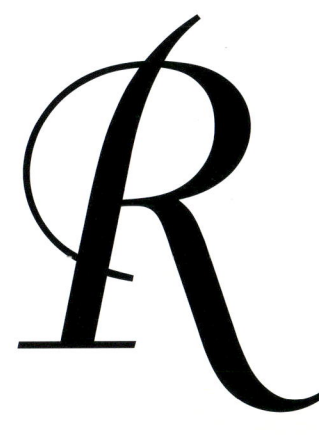 is for Revolution.

Printed copies spread the news across the land. Bells rang. People cheered. Cannons fired. A revolution, or a change in government, was now official. The Revolutionary War would continue until the Americans won in 1783.

...de it at once... fundamentally the Forms of... as abdicated Government here, by declaring... people. — He is at this time transporting large Armies... paralleled in the most barbarous ages, and totally unworthy the Head of a civilized nation. bounty, to become the executioners of their friends and Brethren, or to fall themselves... abitants of our frontiers, the merciless Indian Savages, whose known rule of warfare, is an undistinguished... e Petitioned for Redress in the most humble terms: Our repeated Petitions have been answered only by repeated injury. We... unfit to be the ruler of a free people. Nor have We been wanting in attentions to our British brethren. We... ble jurisdiction over us. We have reminded them of the circumstances of our emigration and settlement here... by the ties of our common kindred to disavow these usurpations, which, would inevitably interrupt our co... consanguinity. We must, therefore, acquiesce in the necessity, which denounces our Separation, and ho... tentions, do, in the Name, and by Authority of the good People of these Colonies, solemnly publish and de... **States**; that they are Absolved from all Allegiance to the British Crown, and that all political conne... that as Free and Independent States, they have full Power to levy War, conclude Peace, contract... States may of right do. — And for the support of this Declaration, with a firm reliance... and our sacred Honor.

We, therefore, the Representatives of the **united States of America**, in General...

Button Gwinnett
Lyman Hall
Geo Walton.

Wm Hooper
Joseph Hewes,
John Penn

Edward Rutledge.
Thos Heyward Junr.
Thomas Lynch Junr.
Arthur Middleton

Samuel Chase
Wm Paca
Thos Stone
Charles Carroll

John Ha[ncock]

Geo...
Rich...
Th...
Ben...
Fra...
Ca...

W. J. STONE SC. WASH^N

S is for Signatures.

Fifty-six members of Congress signed a large handwritten copy of the Declaration of Independence. The British would now be looking to arrest these men for treason against the king.

T is for Timothy Matlack.

Timothy Matlack, the assistant to Secretary Charles Thomson, carefully copied the Declaration.

U is for United States.

With the winning of the war, the United States of America was accepted as a free and independent nation.

V is for Valuable.

Although the Declaration of Independence was to become one of the most valuable documents of the United States, it was not so well cared for in the beginning. It wasn't until 1876 that serious attention was given to its care.

W is for World.

This document sent out a message throughout the world that people had a right to govern themselves.

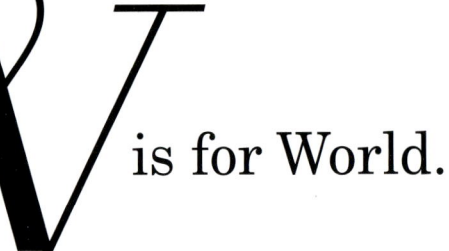

X is in Exhibit.

The Declaration of Independence is now exhibited in the National Archives Building in Washington, D.C.

Y is for Yearly.

Every year many citizens celebrate the Fourth of July with picnics, fireworks, and the reading of the Declaration of Independence.

Z is for Zeal.

Our forefathers loved this country so much that they were willing to fight for its freedom. Thanks to their zeal, or devotion, the United States of America is more than 230 years old.